Clothed in Christ

A study course for naked Christians

Raymond Tomkinson

kevin mayhew

First published in Great Britain in 2008 by Kevin Mayhew Ltd
Buxhall, Stowmarket, Suffolk IP14 3BW
Tel: +44 (0) 1449 737978 Fax: +44 (0) 1449 737834
E-mail: info@kevinmayhewltd.com

www.kevinmayhew.com

9 8 7 6 5 4 3 2 1 0

ISBN 978 1 84417 998 5
Catalogue No. 1501091

Cover design by Rob Mortonson
Edited and typeset by Katherine Laidler

Printed and bound in Great Britain

Contents

This book is dedicated to my darling grandson,
Jacob David Francis Cullen,
in celebration of his baptism

Put on, then,
garments that suit
God's chosen and beloved people:

compassion,
kindness,
humility,
gentleness,
patience.

Be tolerant with one another
and forgiving,
if any of you has cause for complaint:
you must forgive
as the Lord forgave you.

Finally, to bind everything together
and complete the whole,
there must be love.

Colossians 3:12-14

Acknowledgements

Many thanks to the Revd Professor Martyn Percy, Principal of Ripon College, Cuddesdon, and to the Chaplain, the Revd Lister Tonge, who, by inviting me to lead a Quiet Day at the College, inspired this book.

My thanks, as always, to my dear wife Rose, my dear daughter Marian and her lovely husband Rod for the support they give me in all I do.

About the author

Raymond Tomkinson is a priest in the Church of England. Before his retirement due to disability, he was a parish priest in a number of rural parishes and had been, latterly, director of a Christian retreat centre. During the first half of his working life he was a registered nurse specialising in the care of elderly people and in hospice care. He now lives in Rutland with his wife, Rose, and near his daughter and her family. He continues to exercise a ministry of spiritual direction and is a Visiting Spiritual Director to ordinands at Ripon College, Cuddesdon, near Oxford.

His previous books – *Come To Me* (2000), a resource for weary Christians and those who care about them, *God's Good Fruit* (2002), a reflective study course on the fruit of the Spirit, and *God's Advent People* (2003), an Advent course for busy people – are published by Kevin Mayhew.

Introduction

Put on, then, garments that suit God's chosen and beloved people: compassion, kindness, humility, gentleness, patience. Be tolerant with one another and forgiving, if any of you has cause for complaint: you must forgive as the Lord forgave you. Finally, to bind everything together and complete the whole, there must be love. *Colossians 3:12-14*

Those words of St Paul invite us to consider the freedom we have to choose what spiritual garments we wear and how well we wear them. Behind the words we catch a glimpse of the society in which he lived. We know from historical accounts and from archaeological findings that people in the ancient world were as interested in fashion as many people are today. People chose what to put on and they knew what suited them. St Paul relies on that cultural understanding to make a deeper point. He uses the language of fashion as a metaphor to illustrate how we wear virtue to the point that it changes us: making us more like Christ. As we are to 'put on garments that suit God's chosen and beloved people', we might also have to divest ourselves of garments that do not suit us.

This book explores how life experiences can leave us wearing inappropriate and burdensome behavioural garments – how sin, hurt, sorrow, grief and withholding forgiveness can disfigure us, but also how Christ's redeeming love can transfigure us. The sessions describe landmarks in the Christian journey from innocence, through sin and redemption to being clothed in spiritual gifts for living the Christian way of life before we finally come before our Father in heaven, clothed in Christ.

In this book the metaphor of clothing is used in the same way as St Paul used it, to explore the spiritual garments we wear in different circumstances of our lives. Some reference is made to other biblical texts that refer to clothing in a metaphorical or symbolic way. Rather than putting every metaphorical reference to garments and clothing in parenthesis, I have allowed the freedom to switch between metaphorical and physical references to encourage creative thinking around the themes explored.

Use is made of the way in which clothing identifies us or makes statements about us, asking how we relate those external images to the identity we have as Christians: asking ourselves what our spiritual 'clothing' says about us and about our relationship to God, to each other and to the world.

There are suggestions at the end of each session for activities that might help us to explore what our own clothes or spiritual garments say about us and how they manifest emotions, feelings and behaviour towards God and towards other people.

If this book is to be used with a group of people meeting together regularly, group members and individual readers might find it helpful to have a picture of the scene in the Garden of Eden. It could be a photograph of a work of art or simply a mental picture produced by reflecting on the account in Genesis 3.

Also in preparation for the first meeting of a group, members could be asked to bring an item of clothing that they feel says something about them and to use this as a way of introducing themselves. There are suggestions at the end of each session for a 'dress code' for the next meeting.

Those hosting group meetings might like to provide sheets of drawing paper, felt-tip pens or coloured pencils as some of the activities invite people to draw. Instead of a flipchart stand or whiteboard, the group might use either a life-sized outline of a human body, a mannequin or a dressmakers' model on which they could pin slips of paper bearing key words or phrases generated by group discussion. Several of the group activities suggest dressing the model in different ways. A few dressing-up clothes might be useful.

If refreshments are to be served, the food and drink could reflect the theme of the session. Suggestions are given at the end of the preceding session so that people can prepare appropriately.

In addition to prayers for use at each meeting, there are questions which might stimulate discussion about the difficulties of living the Christian life.

For those working through this book alone, the questions for discussion are designed to be thought-provoking. A key scriptural reference is offered as a focus for reflection.

This book is for people of all ages, including those who have completed an adult faith nurture course and want to review their experience of living the Christian life. It might also appeal to teenagers and young adults as the themes discussed can be made accessible through the fashion-related activities, with the potential for light-hearted interaction.

Session 1
Clothed in innocence

Who told you that you were naked?
Genesis 3:11

The story of Adam and Eve in Genesis, the first book in the Bible, is regarded by some as a literal record of how humankind came into being. For others it is a figurative account, written with the benefit of hindsight, not only to make sense of human existence but to identify how humankind developed a propensity to disobey God. This book does not attempt to steer in either direction; rather, we are encouraged to allow the story of Adam and Eve to 'speak' to us afresh: to ask what it might have to say to us about our identity and our relationship with God.

When we study the scene before us we might make a note of what detail draws our immediate attention. Do we see the serpent? Do we see the tree with its forbidden fruit? Artists often portray the fruit as an apple with the intention of attributing sexual overtones to the disobedience. How quickly our attention moves to the fig leaves – the only clothing worn by the archetypal man and the archetypal woman! How quickly, then, we fall in line with historical religious teaching that links sin with sex, and how soon we lose the opportunity to stay with the overall images presented to us of a scene that is meant to show us more than that! Considering that the sin of disobedience was led by what Adam and Eve communicated to each other (with a bit of help from the serpent), it might have been more appropriate for them to have covered their ears, eyes and mouths with fig leaves to hide their shame!

The sin was disobedience and the consequence was that the serpent had been right all along. Adam and Eve did not die because they disobeyed God. Instead their eyes were opened and they, like God himself, knew both good and evil. The implication is that the garden bliss that God had intended for Adam and Eve and their descendants was to be a place where everyone would continue to be innocent, because to know good and to know evil would be to be able to choose between them. God knew his creation so well that he knew that we would, more often than not, choose evil.

Whether we are creationists, whether we are evolutionists or whether we hold another view altogether, the one thing we might all agree on is that having the knowledge of good and evil has brought with it a choice, and our experience of life tells us that it is a daily battle to do good rather than evil. Awareness of the battle within us (we might call it conscience) is only possible because we are self-aware. During those days of innocence Adam and Eve became self-aware. It is clear from their concern to hide their nakedness that they were also God-aware, there being no one else to see their nakedness. Perhaps we have come to believe that one cannot be both God-aware and self-aware but that may not be wholly true.

For the purpose of this reflection on the Adam and Eve tableau, let us try being self-aware in the presence of God, attempting to see what he sees. Once again we may be tempted to believe that God sees us as a disintegrating heap of sin. We will need the help of Jesus and the Holy Spirit if we're going to take an honest look at ourselves. Thanks to his death and rising again, it became possible for Jesus to present us to the Father in the best possible light. It is a form of false modesty to want the Father to see us in a less favourable one!

It can be very hard for Christians to be truly honest before God; to try to see themselves as a loving Father God might see them. The exercise involves coming 'naked' before God, being aware both of the God-given goodness in us and of our faults. Only when we are able to do this exercise in a balanced way will we be able to understand the question God asked Adam and Eve: 'Who told you that you were naked?' Beneath that question is a further question: 'Who told you that you are worth nothing?' 'See,' says the Lord, 'how much I have given you. What you took without permission was the knowledge of good and evil. Now you must accept the consequences of that knowledge and take responsibility for it.'

With the loss of innocence comes self-awareness and personal responsibility. It was time for Adam and Eve to grow up. Who knows, perhaps God had intended to share the knowledge of good and evil with his creation but only when he was ready to give it – only when his children were ready to cope with it.

The first garments worn by humankind are 'God-awareness', 'self-awareness' and 'personal responsibility'. Setting aside all other garments, humankind could make such a difference in the world by wearing those garments well. This is the labour to which Adam and Eve are condemned: to be aware of God (including his loving reproof), of themselves (and their propensity to sin) and of the need to behave responsibly with that knowledge. Responsibility would govern how people would act towards others, how they would teach their children, and how they would act towards the environment. Adam and Eve's eviction from the state of innocence in a garden paradise did not mean that, suddenly, the paradise turned into a giant rubbish tip; humankind managed to do that to great swathes of the earth and the sea all by itself!

The prophet Micah alludes to the basic garments of human behaviour: 'The Lord has told you mortals what is good, and what it is that the Lord requires of you: only to act justly, to love loyalty, to walk humbly with your God' (Micah 6:8).

If you are using this book to reappraise your relationship with God and your neighbour, this might be the time to come 'naked' before God, sobered by Micah's words and by Adam and Eve's experience, and to check out how well those garments of God-awareness, self-awareness and personal responsibility are being worn.

The key question could be: 'Who am I before God?' We ask ourselves this question aware of God's presence and conscious that the light of Christ shines on us. It both illuminates the dark areas of our being and highlights all that is good in us. With this disposition we come naked before God the Father, open and trusting in his mercy. Be aware of the beauty of his creation in and around us. Be aware of all that has been wrought for good in us in spite of our regular disobedience. Be aware, honestly and humbly, that he loves us and that he has endowed us with many gifts and talents.

As we come before God, we pour out the list of sins and failings that have distanced us from him. We must not be daunted by how much we have to pour out nor must we dwell over-long on the exercise. The next exercise may be more difficult: to list the many blessings we have received at God's hand and to give thanks for them. We may want to list the blessings of those who share our life in a special way: our family, friends, neighbours. We may want to include a reference to how blessed we are to have food, warmth, shelter, work, education, security. We might want to list, with deep gratitude, the lifestyle we enjoy. All this we might try to list even if our life is characterised by hurt, pain or disability because these things, too, are part of who we are and we should acknowledge them before God. We do not bring them in the hope of eliciting sympathy but as a statement of fact and an acknowledgement of the context in which we tried and failed, tried and succeeded. In answer to God's question, 'Who told you that you were naked?', we might respond, 'How can I say I am naked when, out of great love for me, you have given me so many spiritual garments to wear?'

Focus for reflection

Who told you that you were naked? *Genesis 3:11*

Questions for discussion

1. How do you read the story of Adam and Eve? Is it literal truth or an allegory to explain human behaviour? Is it something else?

2. Do Christians today focus on the sin of Adam and Eve too much as sexual sin, and so lose the broader understanding of it?

3. Can one be God-aware and self-aware at the same time?

4. How difficult is it to come honestly before God, being aware of our faults, the blessings we have received, and all in the context of our life circumstances?

5. Would you like to recover your innocence?

6. With the Garden of Eden paradise in mind, what more could you do to help protect the environment?

Group activity

Using a piece of coloured paper cut into the shape of a fig leaf, each person writes down key words or phrases that came to them when they reflected on the Garden of Eden scene. The leaves could be made into a garden collage or could be stuck or pinned to a model or lifesize cut-out of the human body to form clothing.

Suggestions for prayer

Lord, I hear you walking in the garden in the cool of the evening
and I want to hide from you
out of shame for having let you down so many times.
I regret the loss of my innocence
but pray that my knowledge of good and evil
will help me to steer clear of wrongdoing
with the help of Jesus Christ our Lord.
Amen.

Lord God, I come before your awesome presence
knowing you to be almighty and all-knowing.
I worship and adore you.
Thank you for creating me and loving me.
Thank you for the many blessings you heap upon me.
May your praise be ever on my lips and in my heart
for the sake of your Son, Jesus Christ our Lord.
Amen.

Loving God, you looked upon all your creation
and it was pleasing in your sight.
Help us to honour you by how we live
and by how we use the resources you have given to sustain us.
Amen.

Key words

Innocence, nakedness, awareness, disobedience, responsibility

Preparation for the next meeting

- Read through the next chapter.

- *Dress code*
  Group members may like to come to the next session wearing what they might wear to a funeral.

- *Refreshments*
  Bring the kind of food you might expect to find at a reception after a funeral.

- *Other*
  Items of first aid equipment might be useful – especially bandages!

Session 2
Mourning clothes

Come to me, all who are weary
and whose load is heavy;
I will give you rest.
Matthew 11:28

We left our virtual Garden of Eden wearing only the clothes we stood up in: God-awareness, self-awareness and a sense of the need to take personal responsibility for our words and actions.

Perhaps Adam and Eve left the garden somewhat sobered by their experience and rather fearful of the life ahead of them: a life characterised by the effects of human frailty. I hope we emerged from our garden reflections in better shape than they did, with a more balanced view of our relationship with God and the world in which we live. We cannot deny that, as Christians, we are at one with God in a way that Adam and Eve were not, but our life on earth is still subject to the same human frailty that they had come to know. We know we are not alone, that God has not left us comfortless. In subsequent sessions we will reflect on the spiritual garments God provides to help us.

In this session we continue to assess our situation, taking a little time to consider what some would call the consequences of humankind's disobedience of God: 'the Fall' that came so soon after we were created. These consequences are sometimes taught as pain, suffering and grief, which is the pain of loss. At some time or other in our lives we will 'wear' the garments of one or more of these human conditions but is this really how God wants us to live? Let us rummage through these everyday garments, these working clothes that we all wear at some time.

Pain is an important signal that something is wrong. It is also a very subjective experience. No one can truly feel someone else's pain, no matter how empathetic we feel we are. The need to communicate our pain to others so that they may help us to relieve it, begins very early in life. Take, for instance, the baby that screams with the pain and develops other symptoms such as dribbling and an upset stomach. A bright red patch might appear on each cheek. Those caring for the child nod wisely and agree that he or she is teething. They try different ways of relieving the pain so that the child is comforted and better able to cope. The child learns about pain and growth. We share their experience because we too have known pain, even though we cannot feel exactly what they feel. We knew about their pain because they wore the garments of distress and suffering, and we recognised them for what they were and tried to help.

In other instances pain and suffering are less easily recognised or understood. We learn how to hide our distress and how to cloak our garment of suffering with stoicism.

Suffering can become more complex as we get older and as layer upon layer of pain and distress is inter-layered with stoicism, and the complicated interaction of medical treatments can further obscure the image we project. This can make it very difficult for those around us to understand what we are going through and how to help us.

Consider the suffering teenager who wears what might seem bizarre and incomprehensible combinations of clothes in an attempt to express themselves or to try out the latest 'look'. How often we see them out in the winter in the skimpiest clothes and in the height of the summer sporting heavy sweaters with sleeves down beyond their hands. Beneath the clothing are garments of confusion and self-consciousness as changes happen to their bodies and emotions. It may well be that the bizarre combinations and choices of clothing signal very clearly what they really feel. Silence and demonstrative outbursts may offer glimpses of many-layered and multicoloured emotional garments that tell of spiritual, emotional and physical suffering. We may find it difficult to help or we may find that what was an appropriate way of helping on one occasion is entirely wrong on another. We may feel frustrated and helpless, sensing the turmoil they are in and not knowing what to do for the best.

It is generally assumed that when we become adults, we all learn, for the most part, to wear our garments of pain unobtrusively, with courage and fortitude. Those who experience chronic, unremitting physical, emotional or mental pain often try, heroically, to get on with their life. There are times, however, when they can only do that if they can demonstrate, from time to time, a little of the pain they wear, eliciting the help and support of others around them.

Sometimes in our congregations there are people who wear their garments of pain and suffering so unobtrusively that no one knows they are wearing them. Sometimes, however, we do not see what garments of suffering people are wearing even when they are obvious. This might be because we feel we are not equipped to help or would not know where to start. Sometimes, the garments of pain and suffering that others wear are not seen because we are so self-absorbed, conscious only of our own problems.

A couple told me about a group which met regularly in their home for prayer and fellowship. During the evening they had shown to the group something of the garment of suffering which cloaked them at that time. On leaving, one of the group gently but firmly warned the couple that people didn't like it when they wore their heart on their sleeve. The couple never again spoke of their suffering in that group. Perhaps William Shakespeare understood better the human need to share these things when he wrote in *Othello*, 'I will wear my heart upon my sleeve for daws to peck at: I am not what I am.'

Some suffering has very obvious external clothing. It may come in the form of a plaster cast that holds a broken bone in place until it heals. The clothing may take the form of disfigurement, the consequence of a fire or car accident. Many have told me that although they have suffered many things in their life, they have received the most sympathy when they wore an outward sign of their pain. One woman told me how she had suffered for many years from a chronic and debilitating illness but, following an accident which resulted in a cast to the ankle, she was inundated with greetings cards, flowers and gifts, all expressing sympathy and pledging help and support.

For many, the everyday garments are the clothes of mourning. Most of us will have known the pain of grief as we have mourned the loss of someone we have loved, but there are other kinds of mourning. We may be mourning the loss of our innocence or the loss of our youth. We may be mourning the loss of our homeland, or of a home we had so carefully provided for ourselves, only for it to be lost in a financial crisis or swept away by flood. Many people bear such loss showing little of it to the outside world, their grieving garments scant and barely perceptible. Some mourning is kept close and private and revealed only to close family members or friends; others will only reveal their grief to a stranger. There are those who can tell no one about the pain of grief they bear except a stranger at the other end of the Samaritans' phone line.

In many societies and in many cultures, grieving is open and shared. People put on mourning clothes as a sign to all that they are grieving. In some cultures the colour of mourning clothes is black and in others it is white. The code is known within the culture and only the stranger may fail to notice. In the days of my youth, people were more inclined to wear black clothes as a sign of mourning. I remember my mother stitching a band of black ribbon to the upper arm of my father's gabardine raincoat following the death of my grandfather. It was a simple sign and one which gave people the opportunity to commiserate or to make allowances if mourners did not seem quite themselves. I have noticed how the colour black has slipped quietly away from mourners, even on the day of a funeral, when it is often replaced by other sombre colours. Occasionally the person who has died has left instructions for there to be no sombre clothes or sad faces at the funeral. Sometimes the rituals of mourning are replaced by celebrations of life with instructions to mourners to come to rites of passage dressed as if for a party. Each of us must determine the 'dress code' for each occasion. Getting the code wrong can add to our own distress and inadvertently cause distress to other mourners.

How, then, should a Christian wear the garments of adversity, suffering, misfortune and grief? Perhaps we feel that even when such garments make an obvious statement of our circumstances (like bandages or a plaster cast), we should accessorise them with unfailing cheerfulness and false bravado. But is that realistic or fair?

More difficult still is that some suffering provides few easily discernible outer garments. Depression, for example, can be difficult to recognise (even by experts in the condition) but there are sometimes clues in the way people sit or move or in the way they lose weight or gain weight. To make matters worse, it can be very hard for people with depression to articulate how they feel. One person described to me that she felt she had been wearing a concrete overcoat for many years and that she didn't know how to take it off.

Some of the garments (or accessories) worn by Christians are worn because the faith community expects them to be worn. Verbal accessories are used to tone down the problems being faced: phrases such as 'It's all good fun' or 'These things are sent to try us' or 'There are others worse off than me' can impress and encourage some fellow sufferers, but they can completely disenfranchise others, making it impossible for them to share how they truly feel about their own troubles. There are times when we might challenge the unfeignedly cheerful 'bling' that attempts to dazzle the observer so that they don't see the garments of pain, suffering and grief. Sometimes we risk the sufferer backing away from us, hoping that we won't be too kind to them in case they break down in tears. At other times our discernment of the true nature of their feelings will be a welcome relief, an opportunity to be helped off with the heavy overcoat of suffering, if only for a short while. As with all our human interaction, we try to be sensitive: seeking God's help to know the time and the place to speak and to know when to be silent and let our actions speak for us.

When we are suffering we may find it hard to believe that anyone really understands, and it may be difficult to hold on to the belief that Christ, out of his great love for us, experienced human suffering and that he wears the garments of suffering with us.

Focus for reflection

Come to me, all who are weary and whose load is heavy; I will give you rest. *Matthew 11:28*

Questions for discussion

1. Does God want us to experience pain, suffering and grief as a punishment for our disobedience?

2. Do you tend to suffer in silence or do you wear your heart on your sleeve?

3. Are the people in your faith community good at noticing and offering help if you are suffering or in distress?

4. Have you ever made it difficult for someone to share their suffering with you by:
   dismissing the significance of their suffering?
   being overly cheerful?
   being too kind?

5. Is there an expectation that we must always be cheerful in adversity? Is that sustainable?

6. How would you like people to be dressed when they attend your funeral?

Group activity

If the group members came as if dressed for a funeral, they might like to share what made them choose particular items of clothing.

Use a model (or even a volunteer!), and ask group members to bandage parts of it and write on the bandages what this silent suffering model might be trying to say to them.

Suggestions for prayer

Lord, we pray to you for those who are in pain.
You know what they suffer.
We call upon you in your infinite mercy,
that you may relieve them of their suffering,
and that they may live to praise your name.
Amen.

Lord, I find it difficult to let people help me when I am feeling low.
Help me to trust those who care about me
and help me to find the right words to describe how I feel.
Amen.

Lord, let my sighs and my tears
speak to you of the sadness in my heart.
Let me feel the touch of your hand upon me,
bringing your healing and your peace.
Amen.

Key words

'Fall', pain, suffering, grief, mourning, empathy, cheerfulness

Preparation for the next meeting

- Read through the next chapter.

- *Dress code*
  People might like to wear their gardening clothes, or something they might consider to be the modern equivalent of sackcloth and ashes, the garments of penitence. They may also like to bring something celebratory to wear (white perhaps) so that they can transform their appearance from mourning to rejoicing by the end of the session.

- *Refreshments*
  Frugal food (reflecting a penitential theme). The host might offer people a small piece of bread and a glass of water on arrival and then serve something celebratory (perhaps a cake with candles) at the end of the session.

Session 3
Robed in righteousness

How could we fail to celebrate this happy day?
Your brother here was dead and has come back to life;
he was lost and has been found.
Luke 15:32

It doesn't seem long since we emerged from the Garden of Eden wearing only enough to cover our modesty, and yet, somehow, we have managed to acquire quite a few layers of everyday garments. I don't know about anyone else but I am finding all these layers quite burdensome. Before we get to the point of divesting ourselves, however, we may have to tolerate one more layer! I like to think of these garments as gardening clothes.

According to the Bible (Genesis 3:16-19, NIV), one of the consequences of the Fall is that we must 'toil'. For the purpose of this reflection we could use the idea of toil to mean the effort we put in to do and say the right thing. It is work we are not very good at doing since we fail at it so often. I am referring, of course, to sin. Whatever the environment in which we live, we find that our spiritual garments get soiled. Here and there on our soiled garments are tears and stains that testify to battles fought and won, or fought and lost. Our garments are soiled, too, by the blows we receive when others sin against us. It is like working in the garden to overcome a wild bramble that is strangling one of our more delicate plants. We wrestle with it and finally overcome it but not without sustaining the odd scratch or cut.

Our attire comprises, too, the shabby garments of self-neglect or the neglect of others. God has given us a truly wonderful body and mind in which our spirit dwells. Should we not respect it and care for it? So often we neglect ourselves or abuse our bodies by working too hard or exercising too little, by what we eat or drink or inhale. These acts of self-abuse take their toll and begin to show.

What a state we are in! Who would recognise us? Fortunately our heavenly Father does.

It is said that a new-born baby looks like its father, even if only for a very short time. This is nature's way of ensuring that the father does not reject the baby but rather forms an attachment to it and so protects it and provides for its needs. Our heavenly Father sees beyond our layers of shabby garments and recognises himself in us and accepts us as his own. After all, we were made in his image and likeness (Genesis 1:26, 27).

What makes us more easily recognisable is when we begin to display garments of regret and remorse. They catch his eye like the effect of waving a white flag of surrender. We catch his attention even from a distance.

In the scriptures there are lots of examples of people covering themselves in sackcloth and ashes, or of tearing at their hair or clothing in a mixture of rage, regret and grief. Perhaps we are less demonstrative in our remorse although, occasionally, one does see such an outpouring of remorse that one fears for the welfare of the penitent. We don't need to do more than have a sincere disposition of regret for what we have done wrong, together with a firm intention to be more faithful to God in the future.

The burden of sin can be a very heavy garment indeed. Christians are not meant to carry a burden of sin, certainly not for very long. We are taught that if we come to God in repentance for our sins, we shall be forgiven. Having come to a state of forgiveness and having made restitution where possible, we are meant to move on with the words of Jesus, 'Go in peace and sin no more', echoing in our ears and with the heavy garments of sin left at his feet.

It can take some people many years to face up to past sin and the long and painful process of remorse can take its toll on them. They may well have begun to wear layer upon layer of garments that have names like 'guilt', 'anger' and 'fear'. Both as a nurse and as a priest I have had the privilege of hearing the unburdening of sin carried for many years and only shed in the last hours of life, and sometimes only then because of a greater fear of meeting God face to face. How little time there can be to tell of God's love and mercy!

Some people are very good at clearing out clothes that are no longer required. Others leave it until the wardrobe is groaning and heaving and the doors are bursting open.

Perhaps this is what the writer of the Letter to the Hebrews had in mind when he wrote, 'With this great cloud of witnesses around us, therefore, we too must throw off every encumbrance and the sin that all too readily restricts us, and run with resolution the race which lies ahead of us, our eyes fixed on Jesus, the pioneer and perfecter of faith' (12:1, 2).

When we come before God in penitence and faith, he looks upon us, dressed as we are. He sees the layers of soiled garments. He sees through each layer right back to the fig leaves and beyond, to his creation marred by sin and toil and suffering and abuse, to the innocent he created out of his great love for us. Jesus could not have made this clearer to us than he did in the parable of the Prodigal Son (Luke 15:11-32).

Remember how the father recognised the wayward son when he was still far off and went out to meet him. There he was, the poor wretched and foolish son, begging at his father's feet. Bruised, battered, bitten by pigs! He was sore, travel-weary, wretched and barely recognisable.

Remember how the father brought him home and called for his finest robe to put round the poor boy to cover his shame. Imagine a tramp covered in sores and filth turning up at the door of a great cathedral, and imagine a member of staff running into the vestry and fetching the finest gold cope, reserved for the bishop (and then only at Easter), and wrapping the poor vagrant in it. I don't think so! Jesus wanted us to know of the father's lavish generosity when the son turned to him in penitence and of our heavenly Father's lavish generosity in forgiving us our sins, never forgetting that we must follow his example and forgive those who sin against us.

This wretched son had left home with half his father's wealth, which was his right in law. He had squandered that wealth and had, effectively, disowned his father, but the father had not disowned him. He called for a ring to put upon his son's filthy finger. By that action he proclaimed to all present that this heap of tatters before them was not to be treated like a slave but that he had, once more, the status of sonship! One can imagine the faces of the household. At least one must have muttered, 'First, he needs a bath!'

Jesus makes his point well that our heavenly Father will welcome us back to him as children and heirs of his kingdom, no matter what state we are in. We too, might think we need a bath first, not least because we would be able to throw off the layers of dark and soiled garments we had acquired before sinking into the refreshing water. In many traditions the rite of baptism models this stripping away of dark garments and, following the rite of cleansing in water, the newly baptised is vested in a white garment to signify the transition from darkness to light, from the death of sin to righteousness of life.

You may remember your own baptism. You may remember occasions when you felt you had shed layers of unwanted and burdensome garments and allowed yourself to be washed by the grace of God and by your own tears of penitence. You may recall how you felt assured of God's forgiveness and emerged from your encounter with God feeling light and clean.

What you will not have found is that you had returned to Garden of Eden innocence. Not only is that not possible but it is not desirable because with innocence comes naiveté. An encounter with sin and the subsequent remorse and acceptance of forgiveness should bring with it a new sense of self-awareness (something, you may remember, that came with the loss of innocence). Your new-found sense of self-awareness should help with resisting temptation in the future and avoiding occasions and circumstances where it would be easy to sin again. Experience is a good teacher and we have much to learn.

As Christians, we know that God sent his Son Jesus to rescue us from the pigsty of our own making and to present us to the Father so that he may wrap us in the cloak of his vast love and mercy, and place upon us the ring of sonship. It is the same cloak with which he covers the earth: the cloak of redemption.

With forgiveness comes the garment of gratitude, which we wear with joy, and the robes of righteousness, which we wear with modesty. They suit us well and they suit our status as children of God. In the world of fashion there is concern that designer garments are copied and passed off as the real thing. We too must beware of imitations! Self-righteousness is a garment to be avoided at all costs. Look at the label! The true robe of righteousness will always point to Jesus and away from ourselves. The robe of righteousness is a gift from Christ, given with love and worn with confidence and joy.

Focus for reflection

How could we fail to celebrate this happy day? Your brother here was dead and has come back to life; he was lost and has been found. *Luke 15:32*

Questions for discussion

1. Robert Burns wrote:

   O wad some Pow'r the giftie gie us
   To see oursels as ithers see us!
   It wad frae mony a blunder free us,
   An' foolish notion.
   ('To a Louse', 1786)

   But does it really help to see ourselves as others see us?

2. Should we make our penitence public or should we keep it hidden?

3. Do you ever find it difficult to believe that your repented sins have been forgiven?

4. How difficult is it to make restitution to a person or an organisation against whom you have sinned?

5. Are you a grudge-bearer?

6. Have you a burden of sin (a concrete overcoat) that you have been wearing for a long time? Can you think what or who God might be sending to help you to remove it?

Group activity

Design a liturgy of penitence and reconciliation that would be acceptable within your congregation.

Suggestions for prayer

God, be gracious to me in your faithful love;
in the fullness of your mercy blot out my misdeeds.
Wash away all my iniquity and cleanse me from my sin.
For well I know my misdeeds,
and my sins confront me all the time.
Amen.
Psalm 51:1-3

Lord, out of the depths I have called to you;
hear my cry, Lord;
let your ears be attentive to my supplication.
If you, Lord, should keep account of sins,
who could hold his ground?
But with you is forgiveness,
so that you may be revered.
Amen.
Psalm 130:1-4

Lord, my heart leaps with joy
when I know that I have been forgiven!
Your victory over sin and death
has brought me life and life in its fullness!
Amen.
Alleluia!

Lord, you wrap your robe of righteousness
around all who call upon your name and seek your mercy.
Help us to forgive others even as you have forgiven us.
May your mercy cloak the whole earth;
for your name's sake.
Amen.

Key words

Regret, remorse, penitence, forgiveness, reconciliation, restoration, restitution

Preparation for the next meeting

- Read through the next chapter.

- *Dress code*
  Wear something you feel really suits you, something you feel good in. Alternatively, bring or wear something you wore to mark a time of transition in your life.

- *Refreshments*
  Bring something unusual or different for others to try.

Session 4
Changing clothes

If you wish to be perfect,
go, sell your possessions,
and give to the poor,
and you will have treasure in heaven;
then come and follow me.
Matthew 19:21

Many clothing stores provide changing rooms so that customers can try on their selected garments to see if they suit them and to see if they fit. The flimsy curtain provides little privacy. The safety of the space might be breached at any moment by a zealous sales assistant appearing suddenly with extra clothes and helpful suggestions such as 'Madam might like to try this in a larger size'! The long mirror can confront us with realities about ourselves that we would really rather not face. Then there is the need to parade in the chosen clothes so that a spouse or friend can offer an opinion. The sales assistant might offer an opinion too, whether or not they have been asked for one!

We might find ourselves thinking, 'Is this really what I want?' We might hear ourselves lamenting the loss of a favourite sweater or jacket so recently given to a local charity shop. Choosing clothes can take time and effort, and changing our wardrobe can hold significance for us that far outweighs all other considerations. Part of us wants things to stay as there are and part of us wants to move on to something new.

Perhaps the story of St Francis of Assisi (1181–1226) may illustrate how changing our wardrobe can be symbolic of changing our life. St Francis was born into a rich family and, like most young people of his station in life, he enjoyed dressing in fashionable clothes made from fine silk, brocade, fur and leather and decorated with semi-precious stones set in gold and silver.

He resisted the idea of following his father into the merchant banking business and considered alternative career paths. He became more and more interested in being a soldier and exchanged his clothes for armour. There were endless wars and skirmishes with neighbouring states and kingdoms so there was always scope for a young man seeking adventure. The young women of his day were attracted to men who lived heroic lives as soldiers. Young men of rich families did not leave their sense of fashion behind. There was no uniform as such, so a soldier of means could have armour made that would flatter him as well as protect him from the weapons of his enemies. Decorated and armour-plated, the dashing young soldier could ride off in a cloud of horse skirts and helmet plumes, leaving the equally fashionable ladies swooning into the arms of their chaperones. That is what Francis Bernardone did.

Some time later, while imprisoned in Perugia, Francis had the opportunity to reflect on his life. He became ill in both mind and body and wore the heavy garments of depression and desperation. He came to understand his long illness as a grace, a rite of passage into a new understanding of himself and of his relationship with God.

On his return home he declared to his family that he would no longer be a soldier and would no longer live the lifestyle of the wealthy classes. His change of heart and his proposed change of lifestyle did not endear him to his father, who had hoped that his son would have returned from his adventures ready to settle down to the family business.

Francis sensed that God was guiding him into making a dramatic gesture to show the seriousness of his intention to live a very different way of life. Carlo Carretto, in his book *I, Francis*, describes the day Francis made that gesture. Francis declares, 'I stripped naked, and flung my clothes into the arms of my father. From this moment forth I am no longer Francis, son of Peter of Bernardone, but Francis, child of God!'

Later Francis would strip naked once again but this time in front of his bishop as he vowed himself to a life of evangelical poverty, taking to heart, quite literally, the exhortation of Jesus: 'If you wish to be perfect, go, sell your possessions, and give to the poor, and you will have treasure in heaven; then come and follow me' (Matthew 19:21). There is something cathartic about such a gesture. Perhaps, at some level and at some time, we might all want to do something like that. We may not feel that we have to take Jesus' words literally. We may feel that it is enough to understand that our possessions are never more important than how we live. Our spiritual garments should always be more precious to us than anything we can buy in a shop.

Certainly this would be the understanding of monks and nuns who live the vowed life. They need shelter, food, clothing and other things if they are to keep well and be able to serve God through their ministry of prayer and service, but they strive to live with as little as possible. It does seem, however, that the needs of ministry have become quite sophisticated these days and a computer or mobile phone might become essential to the task the Lord requires of those who vow to serve him. The key, for them and for us too, is our disposition to wealth and to ownership. What spiritual garments and material clothing have in common is that they are all gifts and not a matter of right or entitlement. God, in his generosity, provides for all our needs so that we are set free to serve him.

We do, of course, have freedom to choose. If we were not free to choose to accept or to reject God or the gifts he offers, we would be slaves rather than being free to love and to serve him.

In the same way that we choose our material clothing, we choose to exercise our spiritual gifts. Everyone at some time neglects the gifts they have been given. Sometimes we are like teenagers who throw a new and much demanded item of clothing carelessly over the back of a chair. If we throw sufficient precious spiritual garments over the back of the chair of carelessness, we quickly lose sight of what we have. Before long we begin to cry, like the teenager, that we have nothing to wear: we believe we have no gifts at all!

From time to time we all neglect the precious gifts and talents we have asked for and have been given. It may be time to dig through the pile of carelessly treated gifts to find among them something very special that we haven't worn for some time. Time for a change does not always mean something new! It may be that we simply need a 'make-over'.

Many people change their clothes to mark a transition from one stage in their life to another. Sometimes, when a relationship is lost, people change their image entirely. For some it is a statement that they are looking forward to a new life. It may be a change that masks the feelings of hurt or loss but it also allows them to present a confident image to the world. Making the effort to change out of old and comfortable clothes that bring a sense of security can be difficult and take huge effort, but it may be a first step to recovery following a time of desolation in our life.

There are other times, too, when people change their clothes to mark significant events in their life. These include receiving Holy Communion for the first time, being confirmed or making another statement of commitment to faith and the service of God. Getting married is a life-changing event, a time of transition, and the bride and groom want to look their best for each other, but they also make a public statement about the significance of the event by what they wear as well as by the vows they make. I am always amazed at the transformation that takes place between the wedding rehearsal and the wedding itself. At the rehearsal the bride may look tired and harassed, her hair falling about her face, her arms folded under an over-large sweater worn with an old pair of jeans, but just 18 hours later she looks like a princess, radiant, coiffured, draped and dressed in her bridal finery. Even her finger-nails have grown a centimetre overnight! She is dressed for transition. Beside her is the bridegroom who has shaved within an inch of his life and is suited and booted and ready for the adventures of married life.

The clothes we wear can also change how we hold ourselves, how we behave. Take a soldier's uniform, for example. Unless the soldier stands erect with head held high, he or she cannot see beneath the peak of the cap!

It was, perhaps, an early-Middle-Ages expression – 'clothes maketh the man' – that inspired William Shakespeare to write in *Hamlet*, 'Costly thy habit as thy purse can buy, but not expressed in fancy; rich, not gaudy; for the apparel oft proclaims the man.' In the same way our spiritual garments show something of who we are. Such garments, such gifts, are not natural but supernatural and, in that sense, somewhat alien to us. It is in the wearing of them that they change us from natural to supernatural beings. They are the garments of Jesus the God-made-man. As we wear them we become more Christ-like, and by becoming more Christ-like we become more like the children God created before we were distracted by a fashion for fig leaves or the gaudy garments of sin.

St Paul describes some of the garments we must put on if we are to become more Christ-like: 'Put on, then, garments that suit God's chosen and beloved people: compassion, kindness, humility, gentleness, patience. Be tolerant with one another and forgiving, if any of you has cause for complaint: you must forgive as the Lord forgave you. Finally, to bind everything together and complete the whole, there must be love' (Colossians 3:12-14).

Thus we will be clothed in Christ. St Paul seems to suggest that if we wear these spiritual garments long enough they will change us. Not only will they *become* us, but they will become *us*!

Underneath this idea of putting on virtue is the hint that it is not natural for us to be compassionate, kind, humble or patient. We know how easy it is to throw off the garments of virtue and to reveal ourselves as far from virtuous. It takes care, effort and some expense to clothe ourselves in virtue but we need not fear because help is at hand. All the garments we need to wear are provided by the Holy Spirit. He is our dresser and it is up to us to wear well the beautiful garments he has given us, but, while it is still a struggle to wear them with ease, the Holy Spirit comes to our assistance. God gives us the grace to become what we wear. We are loved into an elegance that far out-does the best efforts of the world's couturiers!

Focus for reflection

If you wish to be perfect, go, sell your possessions, and give to the poor, and you will have treasure in heaven; then come and follow me. *Matthew 19:21*

Questions for discussion

1. Do you ever feel weighed down by your possessions?
2. Have you a habit of sin that you are reluctant to shed? If so, what would it take to shed it?
3. What spiritual gifts would people say you have?
4. Have you a gift or a talent that you have neglected lately?
5. Do you have a gift or a talent that you are reluctant to use for the benefit of others?
6. The Church is called to proclaim the good news of the kingdom and is constantly trying to find new ways to present an unchanging truth, but is there a danger that we might become slaves to fashion?

Group activity

Create a whole new look for your model by lending some of your own garments. Remember the current fashion for multi-layering!

Suggestions for prayer

O God, my life is cluttered with many things
and the maintenance of them distracts me from serving you.
Help me to re-order my life
and to use all you have given me in your service;
through Jesus Christ our Lord.
Amen.

Sometimes, Lord, I lose sight of the gifts you have given me.
Help me to rediscover the many gifts you have showered upon me
and to nurture them with care,
that I may make a good account of them before you;
for the sake of your Son, Jesus Christ our Lord.
Amen.

Teach us, Lord, to find new expressions of church
that will enable us to proclaim the good news of your kingdom.
Help us to recognise and to affirm each other
in the gifts you have given us,
that we may play our part
in the building of your kingdom on earth.
Amen.

Key words

Changing, transition, gifts, possessions, become

Preparation for the next meeting

- Read through the next chapter.

- *Dress code*
  Wear clothes suitable for a journey. Prepare for difficult terrain or bad weather!

- *Refreshments*
  Bring a small packed lunch, tea or supper.

Session 5
Travelling clothes

My yoke is easy to wear,
my load is light.
Matthew 11:30

Many people have a mirror on the wall in the hall of their home. It is there so we can check our appearance before we leave the house. The bride leaving her parents' home on her wedding day takes one last look in the mirror. The child stands before the proud parent on the first day of term to be brushed off, tidied up and tweaked before being allowed to embark on a new year of education.

We know that we have been restored to life by Jesus and that we have been clothed in garments that befit our status as children of God, but from time to time a mirror is held up in front of us so that we may make sure we are appropriately dressed before we continue on our life journey. It is a time to check that we have understood what God is asking us to do now. What were appropriate garments for yesterday's task may not be appropriate today. It is unlikely that we are being asked to change our whole outfit but a few additions may be required. It is like putting on an apron before preparing a meal, or changing our footwear because the terrain has changed or because we need protection from adverse weather conditions. We are dressing for the next stage of a journey and if we wear the wrong garments, our progress may be hindered.

Much will depend on what we understand God to be asking of us at this time. We may call it 'calling' or 'vocation'. We may need someone to hold up a mirror before us and help us discern our calling. It is a process that can take a very long time. God calls and we respond but the wider church community may help us to make sense of that calling and how best to respond to it. Sometimes the authenticity of a sense of call comes from the people around us offering an opinion: 'Have you thought about becoming a doctor / plumber / pastor?' People might encourage us by saying, 'That job / profession / occupation / way of life would really suit you!'

Here we consider two scriptural texts that are metaphorical references to the garments God's people wear in his service.

The first is the dress code Jesus gave to his disciples before sending them out to proclaim the good news of his kingdom. 'He instructed them to take nothing for the journey except a stick – no bread, no pack, no money in their belts. They might wear sandals, but not a second coat' (Mark 6:8, 9). In a previous session we considered St Francis and his literal response to the Gospel imperative. He and his followers adopted this dress code quite successfully.

There are other references in the New Testament to this image of travelling light. No excess baggage allowed in Christian discipleship!

The reference to travelling and dressing light refers not only to the need to be free to travel unhindered wherever God sends us but to the way the early Christians understood the temporary nature of the Church. The early Christians did not invest in permanent homes or permanent places of worship because they expected Jesus to return in glory at any time. Being on their feet and ready to go had, for Jewish Christians especially, echoes of the Exodus from Egypt. They were ready to go where they were sent at a moment's notice, and equally ready should the Lord return.

There are many people in our world who have only the clothes they stand up in, who live in fear of violent acts of humankind or of nature, and who are ready to flee at a moment's notice to find safety, shelter or freedom. That is not how we would want to live, but neither should we become complacent and so deeply rooted in safety and comfort that we cannot be ready to respond to the Lord's invitation to move on. Most of us are so bogged down with goods, property, commitments, responsibilities and obligations that we could not live with a literal understanding of Jesus' instructions to his disciples. We may feel that his instructions were for a time and circumstances which are not relevant today. We may feel, too, that after two thousand years of waiting for the Lord to return in glory we have mistaken what he intends to do. How, then, are we to honour this scripture?

I suggest it is by looking in the mirror, checking out that we are still dressed appropriately for all he has given us to do. One problem that occurs in church congregations is that people who have served in a particular way for many years have not noticed that it is no longer appropriate for them to continue in the same way. No one dares to tell the faithful steward that while they have kept the church open for 40 years they have also kept it empty! Travelling clothes need adjusting to suit the climate and the terrain if the journey is not to become so arduous that we give up. Those travelling together can be hampered by the one person in the group who has ill-fitting shoes! The message to the first followers of Jesus was clear: travel light. Be ready with your staff in your hand and your sandals on your feet. Be ready to move on – together!

The second scriptural reference is found in St Paul's letter to the Ephesians: 'Put on the full armour provided by God, so that you may be able to stand firm against the stratagems of the devil . . . Fasten on the belt of truth; for a breastplate put on integrity; let the shoes on your feet be the gospel of peace, to give you firm footing; and, with all these, take up the great shield of faith . . . Accept salvation as your helmet, and the sword which the Spirit gives you, the word of God' (Ephesians 6:11-17, abridged).

The idea of weighty armour might seem to contradict the dress code Jesus gave his disciples, but remember he said, 'My yoke is easy to wear, my load is light' (Matthew 11:30). I devoted a whole chapter to this text in my first book, *Come to me.* At that time I was wrestling with the burden of ill health and felt challenged by those words of Jesus. The conclusion I came to then was that sometimes the things that are heavy to carry are only burdensome if they are things we should not be carrying at all.

We are called to put on Christ and to wear him as the armour of God (Romans 13:14), and because it is entirely appropriate that we should do so, there is no weight in our armour at all! Only when we wear the wrong armour is it heavy and burdensome, and the wrong armour includes those things we use to protect ourselves from harm like superstition, lying, defensiveness, deflection and blame. The armour of God, with its component parts of truth, integrity, peace, faith, salvation and the word of God, is so light it can lift us off the ground! When the lifestyle matches the calling, when the inside matches the outside, the armour is weightless and we travel lightly in the service of God. Christ, by his sacrificial love, has taken the weight out of the armour.

Focus for reflection

My yoke is easy to wear, my load is light. *Matthew 11:30*

Questions for discussion:

1. Do you sense that God is calling you to a different way of life or to a different way to serve him? What holds you back? Have other people sensed your call?

2. Are you confused about what God wants you to do next? Who could help you to discern his will for you?

3. If you were called to a place or a state of life that allowed only one small suitcase of clothing and possessions, what would you take with you?

4. Is there anything you do for your church that you should stop doing?

5. Are there people in your congregation who are holding back the work of building the kingdom of God? How can you help them?

6. What kind of armour are you wearing? Is it burdensome?

Group activity

The group imagines that they have decided to form a community and wish to identify themselves as such by adopting a dress code or uniform. The design should reflect their beliefs and values. Each member spends a few minutes working on a design before pooling their ideas.

Alternatively, the group could draw examples of the dress code adopted by Christians or other world religions or factions within them.

Suggestions for prayer

Lord, you knew me before I was formed in my mother's womb
and you have called me by my name.
You call me now to follow your Son, Jesus.
Grant me the grace to hear his call
and the courage to respond wholeheartedly to it;
for his name's sake.
Amen.

Lord, I would follow you wherever you call
but I am weighed down by many things.
Lift from me the burdens I should not be carrying
and, by your Spirit, enable me to carry the burdens
that are part of your will for me;
for the sake of Jesus Christ our Lord.
Amen.

Thank you, Lord, for the people you have sent over the years
to guide me on to the right path.
Thank you for their wisdom and gentle encouragement.
Amen.

Key words

Baggage, burden, calling, discernment, armour

Preparation for the next meeting

- Read through the next chapter.

- *Dress code*
  Come dressed for a wedding.

- *Refreshments*
  Finger food, 'posh nosh'!

Session 6

Wedding clothes

There are three things that last for ever:
faith, hope, and love;
and the greatest of the three is love.
1 Corinthians 13:13

Some of the clothes in our wardrobe come out only on special occasions; others are worn over and over again until they become tatty and misshapen. Even then we are reluctant to throw them out: we have become attached to them.

There are some garments in our spiritual wardrobe that are very special indeed but the difference between these garments and the special clothing in our physical wardrobe is that we are required to wear them all the time, and the more we wear them, the better they look on us. I am referring to the three virtues that St Paul tells us will last forever: faith, hope, and love (1 Corinthians 13:13).

The fashion stylist will tell us that there are basic items of clothing that will suit all occasions and that we need to learn how to wear them with different accessories to suit the occasion. It is the same with these three abiding virtues. I read recently an advertisement in a parish magazine for a talk in the local village hall entitled 'Experiences of a Corset Consultant!' How easily we overlook the foundation garments! The same stylist might tell us that no matter what we wear, it will be worn better if our foundation garments are correct.

Faith, hope and love are the foundation garments of the Christian life. No matter what else has to be thrown out or exchanged, the essentials must remain. We might be tempted to think that we do not need to change at all, but as we have travelled from the Garden of Eden, via the Garden of Resurrection to the places where we encountered the Spirit of God and where we were clothed afresh, we realise that we have changed our garments many times. If we look back over the journey, we see how far we have come. It is like looking at ourselves and each other in an old photograph album. We laugh at the clothes we used to wear. We wonder how we could fit into those clothes or walk in those heels! We have learned to travel light and to carry only those garments that serve us best. Those essential garments of faith, hope and love have not changed beyond recognition but they have been affected by the experience of the journey we have undertaken.

Our faith in God, and in humankind, has been challenged by changes in the Church and in the world, by scandal and trauma. Bad things happen to good people and we wonder why. Our faith has been challenged by the apathy of our fellow-travellers, by their negativity, their unwillingness to change, their self-serving. Our own faith garments are not without spots and stains of a similar kind.

Hope has been challenged as we have sunk so easily into despair when we have seen the rise of secularism, commercialism and greed.

But what challenges love? Surely it is almost everything – and on a daily basis. Everything from the way we conduct ourselves towards others to the way we respond to the needs of the world around us.

Our essential garments, as with all virtue, are attributes of God himself. When we glimpse these garments on others or on ourselves, we glimpse God himself. I reflected on this idea in a previous book, *God's Good Fruit.*

When the Lord returns he will want us to account not for our buildings or our structures but for the state of our faith, our hope and our love: the permanent things, the things that will translate into eternal life. We should remember, though, that faith disappears when we see the reality of God, and hope is dissolved into the realisation of all our true aspirations.

We have dressed for the journey. We have learned something of the need to choose and wear well the garments that suit God's children, to know what is transient and what is, ultimately, of no worth, and how to invest in the virtues of faith, hope and love. We should be dressed and ready for when the Lord tells us to move on to our final destination.

If we find that to be a scary prospect and want to protest that we are not yet dressed for the occasion we might draw comfort from the knowledge we have acquired about God's love, mercy and grace. If judgement came upon us according to how well dressed we are in the gaudy garments of sin, we would all be condemned, but we must remember that it is Christ's robe of righteousness that covers us. Like all the spiritual garments we have been glad to wear, salvation is a gift and not a right.

It is right and proper that we should bear in mind the day when we must account for how we have lived, but we should not dwell too much upon it since we have so much else to do before that day comes. We must focus on the current phase of our journey. When we take a wrong turn or we stumble as we journey along, we need a moment to gather ourselves, to get our bearings and to shake the dust off our garments. As the old song put it, 'Pick yourself up, dust yourself off and start all over again.' We must journey on, not looking back too often and not straining forward too much to see what is ahead.

Over our clothes we wear garlands of joy and gladness, speaking to one another, even through gritted teeth, 'in psalms, hymns, and songs' (Ephesians 5:19). With lightness of heart, even if our steps are heavy, we travel together dressed for heaven like wedding guests gathering outside a church, laughing and chatting excitedly about the prospect of a great day.

Jesus told a story to illustrate something about heaven (Matthew 22:1-14). In the story a king invited many guests to a wedding party but the guests refused to come. Enraged, the king challenged the invited guests about their behaviour but the guests murdered the servants sent by the king. The story was a barely veiled analogy of how God had sent his prophets to tell his ancient people that they were invited to share a blissful relationship with him, but the people had rejected those prophets and continued to resist God's invitation to be faithful. With a reference to those whom God was calling through his own ministry, Jesus continued the story with the account of how the king's servants went out and invited the most unlikely people to the wedding. The story ends on a rather puzzling note. Having invited all the most unlikely people to the wedding, the king throws out one who came without a wedding garment. Jesus makes the point that admission to the wedding party – that is, into heaven – is by invitation and not by right – but what of the wedding garment? Surely it is nothing other than the most important of the spiritual garments that will last forever? Love, the only essential garment for the heavenly banquet because heaven is eternal life shared with Love: the God of love!

As St Paul puts it, 'to bind everything together and complete the whole, there must be love.' (Colossians 3:14). From that love flow compassion, kindness and humility and all the other virtues St Paul did not list on that occasion. We do not stand stark naked before God because we are dressed in our wedding garment but, although we have been clothed with the virtue of love, we do not love perfectly. St Paul, in his great chapter on love (1 Corinthians 13), refers to the way *perfect* love behaves. As frail human beings we have loved less than perfectly but we do not dwell too much on that. Let us be kind to ourselves and to one another, as God is kind to us. We have expressed and professed our love to God and we have demonstrated it by responding to his call and by trying our best to love our neighbour as ourselves. We wear love as a garment and in the wearing of it throughout our lives, love *becomes* us. Love becomes *us*!

When we arrive at the entrance to the wedding feast of heaven, it will be Christ the heavenly Bridegroom who will welcome us. He will present us to the Father. We will come before him with a disposition of openness and trust, hiding nothing, boasting of nothing. We have come before the Father who created us in love, and he will gaze upon us even as we gaze upon him. We will have allowed the Son to bathe our wounds and cover our shame and cloak us in the wedding garment of his redeeming love.

Even though that will be the final outcome, we will need to make the effort to wear love for each other in compassion, kindness and humility. An American television interviewer at an Oscars ceremony asked arriving guests, 'Who are you wearing?' In the same way, we must remember whom we wear: none other than the King of heaven, because we are clothed in Christ!

Who told you that you were naked?

Focus for reflection

There are three things that last for ever: faith, hope, and love; and the greatest of the three is love. *1 Corinthians 13:13*

Questions for discussion

1. Does the company of other Christians always feel like a wedding party gathered excitedly in anticipation of *the* great day? If not, why not?

2 If a passer-by saw you gathering outside church before or after a service, would they think you were there for a wedding, a funeral or something else?

3. Are there people who wear virtue well and whom you admire and seek to emulate?

4. We are called to live by faith but what is the opposite of faith? Doubt? Certainty? Or something else?

5. Hope is a virtue, but is it also a discipline?

6. What makes it difficult for you to love your neighbour?

Group activity

Imagine your model is the universal Church and dress the model as the Bride of Christ. Alternatively, dress the model as a Christian clothed in Christ, ascribing Christian attributes and virtues to items of clothing, footwear or armour.

Suggestions for prayer

Father God, you created us out of love
and have shown us your great love for us
by sending your only Son to redeem us.
He kept his promise and sent your Holy Spirit
to plant your love deep in our hearts.
Let your love grow in us,
and help us to show your love to the world;
for Jesus Christ's sake.
Amen.

Lord Jesus Christ, you opened wide your arms on the cross
to embrace us all.
Help us to demonstrate your love to the world.
Amen.

Holy Spirit, clothe us afresh in the gifts of faith, hope and love,
that we may become more and more like Christ Jesus
to the glory of God the Father.
Amen.

Key words

Foundation, wedding garment, faith, hope, LOVE!

Summary

The final preparations for a wedding can be hectic, leaving neither bride nor bridegroom with an opportunity to pause for reflection. Those who prepare couples for marriage and writers in secular magazines all urge the bride and groom to find a few moments to pause and to reflect on what has brought them to their 'big day'. More than anything else it will have been love. It is the foundation of their relationship and will be the foundation of their life together.

In the same way, we may reflect on our own journey of faith from the garden of innocence, through sin and redemption, putting on spiritual garments so that we are appropriately dressed to bear witness to Christ in this world and be presentable to the Father in the next. We may reflect, too, on how wearing Christ has changed us, how, marvellously, and through God's love for us, we have become what we wear.